Sunflowers
and
Friendships:

A Lesson in Patience

Marcy Schaaf

Dedication

To my sister Laura,

For sharing this funny true story and inspiring this heartfelt tale. Your love for sunflowers and your unwavering patience taught me a valuable lesson about life and friendship. Thank you for always being a source of laughter and inspiration. This story is as much yours as it is mine.

Love you more,
Your little sister

Laura loved sunflowers. She dreamed of a
big sunflower field.

"One day, I'll have my own sunflower field,"
she said.

She imagined bright yellow sunflowers
everywhere.

Laura decided to make her dream come true.

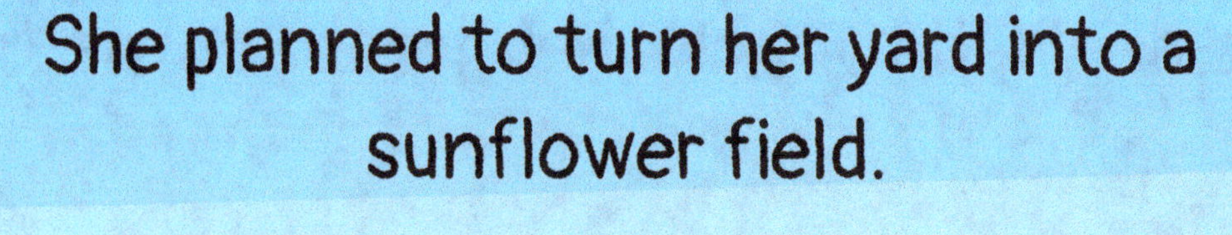

She planned to turn her yard into a
sunflower field.

First, Laura removed the grass by hand.

She used a shovel, working hard every day.

Next, she rototilled the dirt to loosen it up.

Laura added compost to the soil.

She knew it would help her sunflowers
grow strong.

Then, she planted 400 sunflower seeds carefully.

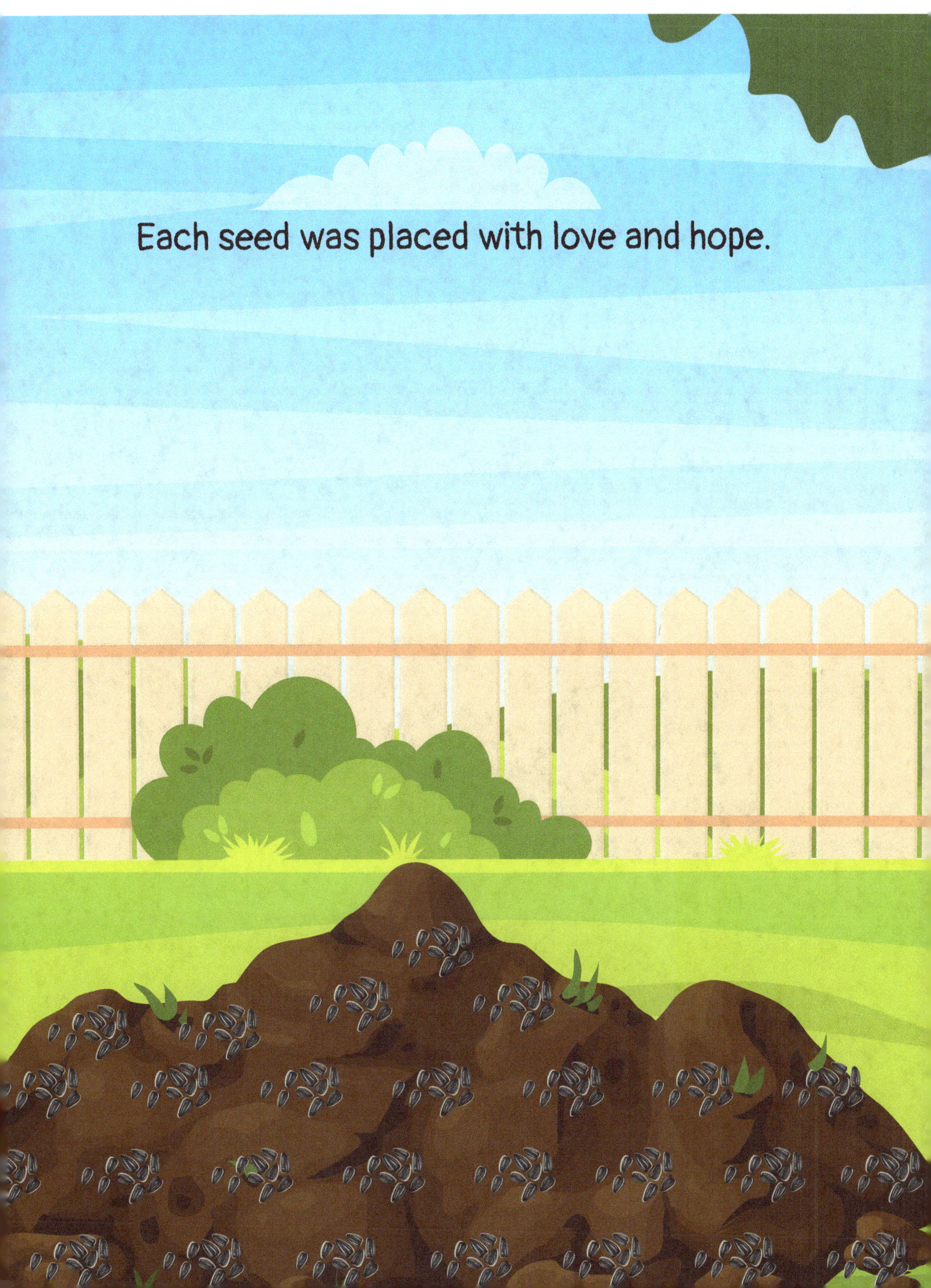
Each seed was placed with love and hope.

Laura watered the seeds every day.

She watched and waited for them to grow.

Laura was excited and kept caring for them.

One day, Laura noticed weeds growing.

She started weeding the sunflower field.

Hours passed as she pulled out the weeds.

Laura was proud of her hard work.

But something didn't seem right.

She researched on her phone.

Laura was shocked!
She had pulled out the sunflowers.

She realized she had left the weeds.

Laura felt sad and frustrated.

She learned she needed to be patient.

If she had waited, she could tell the difference.

Just like with sunflowers, people need time too.

We need patience to see who will be a true friend.

Be aware of red flags like unkindness or dishonesty.

With patience, you will find
the best friends for you.

The End

This true story is about my sister Laura
see how unhappy she looks after pulling
all the sunflowers out!

Books By Schaaf

www.BookBySchaaf.com

Find us at: